MEDITATE

Happiness Lies Within You

MEDITATE

Happiness Lies Within You

by

Swami Muktananda

CSP

A SIDDHA YOGA PUBLICATION
PUBLISHED BY CHITSHAKTI PUBLICATIONS, CHENNAI

First reprint of 1999 edition published in India in 2005 by Chitshakti Publications (a division of Chitshakti Trust), Chennai, under licence from the copyright holder.

Original language: Hindi

Printed by Infomedia India Ltd., Mumbai.

For sale only in India, Nepal, Bhutan and Sri Lanka.

ISBN: 81-86693-42-4

Contents

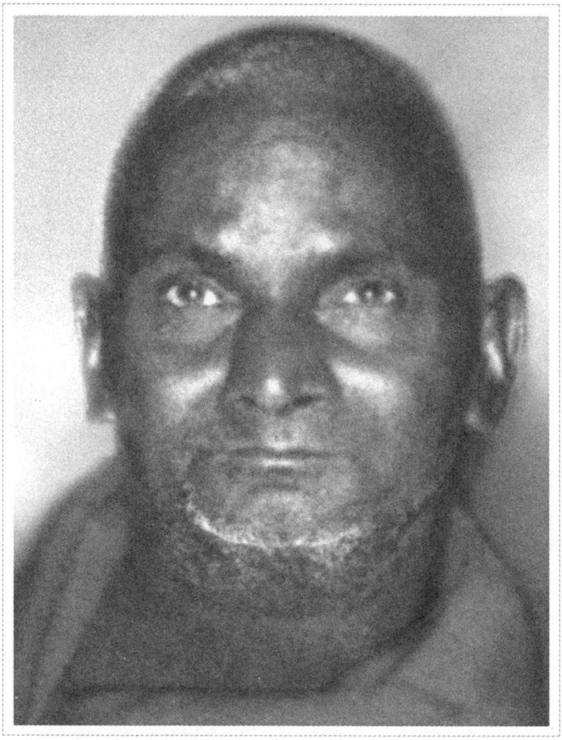

Bhagawan Nityananda,
Swami Muktananda's Guru

SWAMI MUKTANANDA
And The Siddha Yoga Lineage

A string of refulgent beacons adorns and illuminates the spiritual firmament. They are the Siddha Yoga Masters, Selfrealized beings who have been vanquishing the forces of darkness and ignorance since time immemorial. Manifesting in the world in an unbroken lineage originating in Lord Shiva himself, they are the living embodiment of God's Grace.

Through the gift of Shaktipat Diksha, such a Master awakens in his devoted disciple the inner, dormant spiritual energy, known as Kundalini. Shaktipat initiates a great yoga — Siddha Yoga — which leads to profound inner transformation and eventual Self-realization — the highest goal of human life.

Once a Self-absorbed and supremely serene Siddha came to a secluded valley in Maharashtra, fifty miles north-east of Bombay. He settled there in the hamlet of Ganeshpuri and within a short period of time it was as if the land had been touched by a Philosopher's Stone. Whoever appeared before the august presence of that great avadhut, Bhagawan Nityananda, found his problems solved, his desires fulfilled, and his mind peacefully resting in God.

One day a wandering sannyasi, Swami Muktananda, joined the multitude of devotees who gathered to seek the darshan and blessings of Bhagawan Nityananda. Swami Muktananda's coming was an event of such magnitude that it turned a new golden leaf in the spiritual history of India and the whole world.

Swami Muktananda was born in 1908 in Mangalore, Karnataka. As a young boy he had an insatiable thirst for hearing the life stories of the saints and a great yearning for their company. He little knew the profound effect such company could have on an earnest seeker! For after receiving the blessings of a young wandering avadhut, the fifteen-year-old boy found himself becoming increasingly restless.

Although he was surrounded by material affluence and the overflowing love of his family, the bonds of pleasure and affection were loosening and falling away and the outer world of family life was dissolving. With a heart set afire with his desire to know God, he left his home in search of a Master who could give him the direct experience of the Truth.

His first stop was the ashram of Siddharudha Swami, and it was here that he took the vows of sannyasa and was given the name Swami Muktananda — the Bliss of Freedom. Over the next twentyfive years, the young swami travelled all over India on foot. He mastered the scriptures and became proficient in hatha yoga, ayurvedic medicine, and many other branches of learning. His spiritual longing became more and more intense. but although he met more than sixty great saints, nowhere did he find the Truth he sought.

Those were days of searching self-enquiry, self-purification, and the practice of intense austerities. The young sannyasi faced many arduous tests, often going without food and adequate clothing.

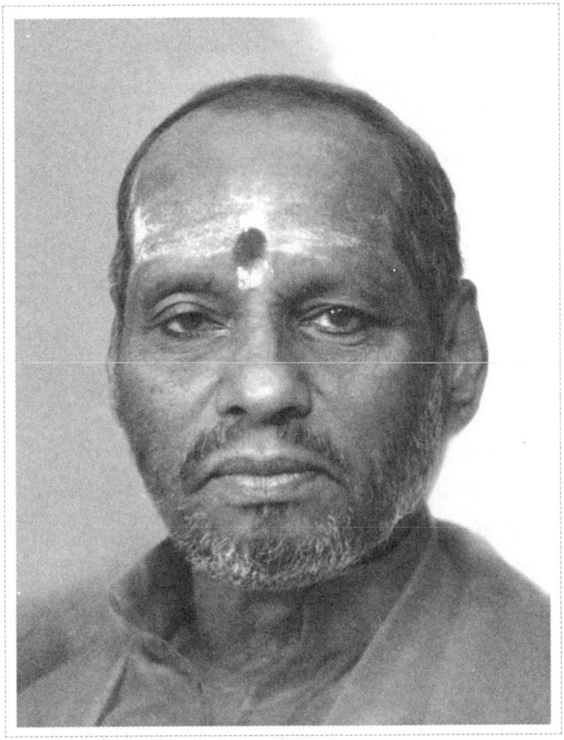

Swami Muktananda

But his search for a Master was coming to an end. With a heart pure like molten gold, Swami Muktananda came to Ganeshpuri and found refuge in the feet of Bhagawan Nityananda, the very same avadhut whose blessing had initiated his search so long ago in his boyhood.

Through Bhagawan Nityananda's grace-bestowing power, Swami Muktananda received a supremely divine Shaktipat on 15th August, 1947, the same day that India received her freedom after so many struggles. This divine initiation put an end to his spiritual restlessness and set him on the path of inner pilgrimage. For the next nine years, he went through extraordinary transcendental experiences, often in remote and solitary places. His intense meditation brought him ever closer to the door of Self-realization.

Finally, in 1956 he reached the goal of his rigorous sadhana and became established in the inner Self. At that time, far away in his room in Ganeshpuri. omniscient Bhagawan Nityananda started dancing with joy, shouting: "Muktananda has become the Absolute! Muktananda Paramahamsa!"

Bhagawan then installed the Self-realized yogi in a small house on a site one mile down the road from Ganeshpuri. and here Baba — as he came to be known — tended the garden and talked to devotees sent to him for spiritual instruction by Bhagawan. For five years he lived the life of the perfect disciple, laying the foundations of the future Gurudev Siddha Peeth Ashram.

Before taking Mahasamadhi and becoming eternally one with the Absolute, the living Guru bequeaths to his chosen disciple the full power and authority of the Siddha Yoga

Gurumayi Chidvilasananda

lineage. Thus commanded, the chosen disciple himself becomes the Sadguru. In 1961, just before taking Mahasamadhi, Bhagawan Nityananda bestowed that power and authority on Swami Muktananda, including the capacity to give Shaktipat.

The following decade saw the stream of seekers from India and abroad who came for spiritual knowledge become a wide river. Informed by the divine wisdom of his own supreme attainment, Baba expounded for them the path of the ancient lineage of Siddha Yoga Masters, a yoga which was uniquely suited to the spiritual needs of twentieth-century seekers. He instructed his devotees in the eternal Truths of the ancient scriptures and in the spiritual practices of the classical yogas.

In 1970, Baba Muktananda set out on the first of his three World Tours, bringing the nectarean experience of the Truth to thirsty seekers in other lands. As a spiritual magnet, he was supremely powerful and irresistible, initiating a great "Meditation Revolution." He wrote over thirty books, gave countless talks, designed many special programmes, and everywhere presented his timeless message:

Meditate on your own Self.
Honour your Self.
Worship your Self.
Understand your Self.
God dwells within you as you.

Guided by the inner command of Bhagawan Nityananda, the gigantic wheel of Baba's unique Meditation Revolution moved ever faster. He established meditation centres around the globe, and gave Shaktipat initiation to many thousands of seekers. Never before had this secret and well-guarded gift been made available on such a grand scale. A new spiritual map of the world was being drawn, and Baba Muktananda was becoming widely acclaimed and honoured.

At the same time, a divine plan was unfolding with thrilling and far-reaching consequences. A brilliant and extraordinary girl had been visiting the ashram to sit at Baba Muktananda's feet. From the earliest years, Baba knew her greatness. When she was still a young girl, he said of her, "She is a great flame. One day she is going to illumine the whole world."

In 1974 Baba took his young disciple travelling with him on his second and third world tours, and over the years she translated his books, talks, and conversations. Through her devoted service to her Guru, through intense spiritual discipline and rigorous study of the scriptures, this supremely deserving disciple was preparing for her great destiny. Finally, crossing over all the hurdles and tests, she attained the highest illumination.

A short time before taking Mahasamadhi, Baba Muktananda formally gave her sannyasa and the name Swami Chidvilasananda — the Bliss of the Play of Consciousness. He also conferred on her the power and authority of the Siddha Yoga Lineage. On October 2, 1982, Swami Muktananda took Mahasamadhi.

Affectionately known as Gurumayi — 'one who is absorbed in the Guru'— Swami Chidvilasananda continues the mission of her Guru, guiding sincere seekers in the ancient path of Siddha Yoga.

In this stress-ridden modern world, Shri Gurumayi is an immovable support, a powerful and unfailing boat to take us across the turbulent waters of life. She is the Ganges of wisdom for those who are thirsty for knowledge and the door to liberation for yearing seekers. Through her, the radiant light of spiritual power dwelling in the Siddha Yoga Lineage continues to illumine the world.

Foreword

The release of the book MEDITATE in India will be of great benefit not only to followers of Siddha Yoga Meditation, but to spiritual seekers in general. It is the rare and invaluable gift of a Siddha Guru. The book does not address itself to those who are merely intellectually curious; it opens the door to those who have the courage and the yearning to plunge themselves into the world of Light, the world of Love, the world of Truth. The meditation practised, mastered and taught by Swami Muktananda, opens the doors which lead to the ultimate goal of our existence — to Self- realization.

From time immemorial, man has sought to be at peace with himself and the world around him, to come to terms with the mysterious and, in large measure, unknown universe. Seekers have expressed these concerns as questions, and sages and seers have uncovered the answers within themselves through meditation, bringing solace and spiritual comfort to mankind.

This book MEDITATE contains Baba Muktananda's essential teachings on meditation. Here he not only tells us why we should meditate, he also teaches the techniques of meditation that he himself practised. To quote from the book, "We do not meditate to relax a little and experience some peace. We meditate to unfold our inner being." The object of human life is to seek the Inner Self through meditation and other spiritual practices and to discover that this inner Self is identical with God.

In explaining meditation, Baba uses the four wheels of a car as a metaphor. The first wheel is focus on the inner Self; second is use of a mantra, a word or syllable that assists concentration; third is *āsana* or the sitting posture that supports the body steadily and comfortably; and fourth is the breath, balancing the twin processes of inhalation and exhalation.

However, Baba tells us that the easiest way to meditate is through the awakening of the *Kundalinī* energy lying dormant in every human being. To do that, we need to receive the grace of a spiritual Master whose own power has been awakened by his own Guru, and who has been empowered to give Shaktipat to others. Then meditation is not an arduous activity, Baba says, but can happen as easily as sleep. "When the Guru's power is transmitted into us and awakens our inner dormant power, meditation comes to us spontaneously on its own."

Siddha Yoga Meditation is a way of life that can be practised while engaged in our daily activities, whether pursuing our vocation or profession or doing our household chores. That is why Siddha Yoga Meditation is so appropriate for the modem age.

This powerful book has played a significant role in bringing about the meditation revolution that was initiated by Baba Muktananda, and is being brought to fruition by Swami Chidvilasananda, the current Master of the Siddha

Yoga lineage. Gurumayi, as she has come to be known throughout the world, has turned it into a global movement, giving spiritual guidance and the transforming experience of meditation that opens people up to connect with this Inner Self, the source of divine joy.

Gurumayi tells us to look to the God that is within, and then to perceive that same divinity in all other human beings. Through this process we will become full of love, humility, fellow feeling, and innate goodness. The world around us will be transformed into a better place to live in.

My first meeting with Gurumayi was on 31 st March, 1988. She has had a profound influence on my life ever since. I had always taken an interest in the Upanishads and in the teachings of our saints, but since meeting Gurumayi, spirituality has become an essential part of my daily life. I am deeply touched to see how she teaches people, transforming them into better human beings, with love and respect in their hearts for others.

The process of transformation can start with reading MEDITATE. Apart from making the complexities of meditation simple and accessible to the common man, the words of the book themselves carry the Guru's grace.

Dr Nitish Sengupta

Delhi, 1993

MEDITATE

Happiness Lies Within You

MEDITATE ON THE SELF

IN THE UPANISHADS there is a question: What do human beings want? The answer is that we want happiness. Everything we do, we do for the sake of happiness. We seek that happiness through our work, through our friends and family, through art and science, through food, drink, and entertainment. For happiness, we perform all the activities of daily life, and this is why we keep expanding our material world.

Inside us lies divine happiness, the same happiness we are looking for in the world. If we think about the joy we derive from different activities, we will realize that we experience happiness not in the activities, but within ourselves. For example, when you look at a beautiful picture, where do you feel pleasure, in the picture or in yourself? When you eat a delicious meal, do you experience satisfaction in the food or in yourself? When you meet a friend and feel joy, is that joy in your friend or in yourself? The truth is that the joy you find in all these things is simply a reflection of the joy of your own inner Self.

The testimony for this is our sleep. At the end of every day, no matter how much we have eaten or drunk or earned or enjoyed, we are exhausted. All we want to do is to go into our bedroom, turn off the light, and take refuge in a blanket. During sleep, we are completely alone. We do not want our wife, our husband, our friends, our possessions. We do not eat anything, we do not earn anything, we do not enjoy anything. Yet while we are sleeping, the weariness of our waking hours is removed independently, by the strength of our own spirit. In the morning when we wake up, we feel completely rested.

This is an experience that we have every day. If we think carefully about why we become exhausted from everything we do during the day and why we get so much peace from sleep, we will understand that the real source of our contentment is not eating or drinking or anything outside ourselves, but is within. During the day, the mind turns outward. However, in the sleep state, the mind takes some rest in the Self, and it is this which removes our fatigue. Absorbed in the little bliss of sleep, we forget the pains of the waking state. If we were to go just beyond sleep and enter into the state of meditation, we would be able to drink the nectar of love and happiness that lies in the heart.

That nectar is what we are looking for in all the activities of the outer world. What we are really seeking is the supreme Truth, and through meditation we can experience that Truth vibrating in the form of sublime happiness in the heart.

Truly speaking, a human being is divine. It is only our wrong understanding that keeps us small. We think of ourselves as the body. We think that we are a certain physical structure, with hands, feet, legs, and eyes. We think of ourselves as a man or a woman, as belonging to a particular class or country. We identify ourselves with our thoughts, our talents, our good or bad actions. But none of these things is what we are.

Within us is a being who knows all the actions of the body and the mind and remains untouched by all of them. In the *Bhagavad Gītā,* Lord Krishna says: "Arjuna, this body is called a field, and the one who knows it is called the knower of the field."[1]

The one who knows the field must be different from the field. For example, one who says "my book" must be different from the book; one who says "my table" must be different from the table. In the same way, one who says "my body" must be different from the body; one who says "my mind" must be different from the mind. Who is that being who observes the activities of our waking hours? At night when we go to sleep, that being does not sleep, but stays awake and in the morning reports to us on our dreams. Who is that knower? In the *Gītā,* Krishna answers this question: "O Arjuna, I am the knower of all these fields."[2]

The one who lives in the body, but who is apart from the body as the knower of it, is our real Self. That Self is beyond the body, beyond the mind, beyond distinctions of name, color, and sex. It is the pure "I," the original I-consciousness that has been with us since we came into the world. We have superimposed different notions onto that I-awareness, notions like "I am black," "I am white," "I am a man," "I am a woman," "I am American," "I am Indian." Yet when we wipe away those superimpositions, that "I" is nothing but pure Consciousness, and it is of the form of bliss. It was with the awareness of that "I" that the great Shankaracharya proclaimed, *"Aham brahmāsmi,* I am the Absolute."[3] That "I" is God, and we meditate to know That directly. As we see it more and more, we become transformed.

There are many techniques that are supposed to lead us to God, but of all these, meditation is the one recognized by all the saints and sages, because only in meditation can we see the inner Self directly. That which lives in the heart cannot be found in books. If we look for it in churches and temples, we cannot find it. Logical reasoning and the ability to give great lectures are of no use either. Since that being is our innermost Consciousness, it is necessary for us to turn within to have a direct experience of it.

There was a time when I was addicted to reading the scriptures. One day I went to see my Guru with a book under my arm. He said, "Muktananda, come here. What is that?"

"It's an Upanishad," I replied.

"Do you know how this book was made?" he asked me. "It was made by a brain. The brain may make any number of books, but a book cannot make a brain. You had better throw it away and meditate."

So I threw the book away and began to meditate. This makes perfect sense. When the Self is within, why should we look for knowledge of it somewhere else? As long as we do not realize the Self within, we cannot find true peace. We can never be happy, no matter how much we have in the outside world. So meditation has the highest importance; it is necessary for everyone.

The Upanishads say that everything in the universe is in meditation.[4] The earth is held in position by meditation, fire burns through the power of meditation, water flows through the power of meditation, and the wind blows through the power of meditation. Through meditation, the ancient sages discovered the various laws of society and how to govern so that everything functioned smoothly. In the same way, the secrets of the ancient sciences were revealed to these sages. Through meditation, they accomplished great tasks.

Meditation is universal. It is not the property of any particular sect or cult. It does not belong to the East or to the West, nor does it belong to Hinduism, Buddhism, or Sufism. Meditation is everyone's property, just as sleep is everyone's property: it belongs to humanity. Meditation is not something difficult or strange. All of us, in our daily lives, are already familiar with it. Without meditation, a doctor could not diagnose a disease, nor could a lawyer prepare a brief, nor a student pass an examination. All our arts and skills, from driving a car to cooking a meal to painting a picture to solving a mathematical problem, are perfected through the power of concentration, which is nothing but meditation. However, these are external forms of meditation. When we turn our attention within and focus on our inner being, just as we focus on external objects, we are meditating on the Self.

Meditation is such a great purifier that it washes away the sins of countless lifetimes and removes all the impurities and tensions that beset the mind. Meditation rids us of disease and makes us more skillful at everything we do. Through meditation, our inner awareness expands, and our understanding of inner and outer things becomes steadily deeper. Through meditation, we travel to different inner worlds and have innumerable inner experiences. Above all, meditation stills the mind—which constantly wanders, which constantly causes suffering—and establishes us forever in the state of supreme peace, which is independent of any external factors. Ultimately, meditation makes us aware of our own true nature. It is this awareness that removes all suffering and delusion, and this awareness comes only when we see, face-to-face, our own inner Self.

If even once we could see the Self as separate from the body, we would understand that the body does not bind us, that the pains and pleasures of the body do not affect us. According to the seers of Vedanta, pain and pleasure affect only a person who does not know the inner Self.[5] Even in daily life, we know that we experience physical pain and pleasure only for a certain length of time and only in a certain state of consciousness; we do not experience them at all times or in all states. For example, if a person has a boil on his hand, it hurts during the day, but as soon as he goes to sleep, he stops feeling the pain. A person may have a nightmare in which he sees a tiger rushing at him, and he may become frightened and scream, "Save me, save me!" But when he awakens, the tiger is nowhere around, and he realizes that he has only been dreaming.

So the pleasures and pains of the dream state do not reach the waking state. In the same way, the state of meditation is beyond the pleasures and pains of the waking, dream, and deep-sleep states. In meditation, we become the witness of all our states. This is the state of God, of the inner Self, and through meditation we can attain that state because it is within us. When we pass from dream to waking concious-ness, our understanding of ourselves changes. In the same way, when we reach the state of the Self, we understand ourselves differently: we understand that we are divine.

There was a great being named Hazrit Bayazid Bistami. He was a Sufi who used to pray and meditate continually. As his meditation became deeper, he reached a state in which he began to proclaim, "I am God, I am God." One who has not experienced that state may find it hard to understand, so I will explain with a simple analogy. You know from your own experience that your idea of yourself keeps changing as your consciousness changes. A policeman, as long as he is an ordinary policeman, will keep saying, "I am a policeman." When he becomes a captain, he will stop saying, "I am a policeman," and say, "I am a captain." And when he becomes a commissioner, he will say, "I am a commissioner." As long as a person is studying, he says, "I am a student," but when he finishes his studies and begins to teach, he says, "I am a teacher." The same "I" is experiencing all these states. When that "I" which identifies itself with the body in the waking state, saying, "This body is mine," or "I am a policeman," or "I am an American," passes from the level of waking consciousness to the highest, subtlest level of consciousness, it attains this awareness: "I am God." That understanding emanates from the deepest place inside us.

When a river flows into the ocean and becomes one with the ocean, it is no longer a river; it is the ocean. In the same way, Hazrit Bistami would reach a state in which he would experience himself as all-pervasive Consciousness, the highest Truth, and he would shout, "I am God." He did not know what was happening to him, and he could not pass into this state at will.

Although he was a great being, Bistami's teachings had always been the orthodox teachings of Muslim priests. He would tell his students, "Pray to God, be forgiven for your sins. God is somewhere up above." So when Bistami began to shout during meditation, "I am God, I am God," his students were shocked. When he came out of his room, they surrounded him and cried, "Bistami, you are guilty of a terrible heresy! We cannot understand what is happening."

Bistami said, "Please tell me, what sin have I committed?"

The students explained, "We could hear you exclaiming from inside your room, 'I am God, I am God.' How can a human being, who is corrupt and sinful, be God? That goes against the holy law of Islam."

"I am not really to blame for this," Bistami told them. "When I am in meditation, I am not in control of what I say. If you hear me say these things again, you can punish me in any way you like."

The students agreed. After about a week's time, Bistami again sat in meditation. This time he began to shout louder than ever, "I am God, I am God, I am God! This earth has come from me. I am the mountains and all the oceans. I flow as water in the rivers. I am everywhere. I am in the West and the East; I am in the North and the South; I am above and below."

When the students heard Bistami shouting in this way, they thought he had become completely insane and rushed to get weapons in order to silence him. As soon as Bistami came out of his room after meditation, the students grabbed him and began to beat him.

There was only one of him, and there were so many students. What could he do? So, once again, he sat down. The moment he touched the ground, he glided into meditation and began to proclaim, "I am God, I am God. Whatever there is has emanated from me. Fire cannot burn me, water cannot wet me, and bullets cannot kill me. I am in that state which is beyond everything. I am the highest of the high. Death cannot come anywhere near me. I am That which is the supreme Lord."

As the students were stoning and beating Bistami, an amazing thing happened. The punishment they were inflicting began to rebound onto themselves. The student who had been hitting Bistami's head found his own head being hit. The one who had struck his arms found his own arms hurt. Another who had been beating his legs found his own legs broken. Finally, for their own sake, the students stopped beating Bistami and sat down.

Bistami was still shouting, "I am God, I am God," but the students did not want to take another chance. They sat at a respectful distance, not daring to go anywhere near him. After a while, Bistami came out of meditation, and the students said to him, "Sir, we don't understand what has happened. Our legs and arms are bleeding. Our heads are broken. We thought we were hitting you, but we ended up hitting ourselves."

Bistami said, "When I was in meditation, when I was in that state, I was no longer Bistami. I was the highest goal of your religion. I was all-pervasive, and if anyone hits a being in such a state, it is like hitting one's own Self. That is why the blows bounced back onto you."

This is the state that we are supposed to attain in meditation. We do not meditate only to relax a little and experience some peace. We meditate to unfold our inner being. The *Brihajjābāla Upanishad* says: Through meditation, we reach a place where the wind does not blow, where the heat of the sun does not reach, where death cannot penetrate.[6] This is the country of eternal bliss. If a yogi becomes established there, he becomes liberated. Death cannot touch him.

SHAKTIPAT

MEDITATION ON THE SELF is not difficult. The real secret of meditation is shaktipat, the inner awakening that takes place through contact with a Siddha Guru. Within every human being lies a great and divine energy. The Indian scriptures refer to it by different names, such as *shakti* (supreme energy) or chiti (universal Consciousness), and when it resides within a human body, this conscious energy is known as *kundalinī*. This inner power is the same creative force which is responsible for the creation, sustenance, and withdrawal of the world. The *Pratyabhijñāhridayam,* one of the essential texts of the great spiritual philosophy Kashmir Shaivism, describes this energy in an aphorism: "Universal Consciousness creates this universe in total freedom."[7]

Contemporary scientists are becoming aware that the basis of the universe is energy. They are discovering what the sages of India have known for millennia: that it is Consciousness which forms the ground, or canvas, on which the material universe is drawn. In fact, the entire world is the play of this energy. Within its own being, by its own free will, it manifests this universe of diversities and becomes all the forms and shapes we see around us. This energy pervades every particle of the universe, from the supreme Principle to the tiniest insect, and performs infinite functions. Yet even though it becomes the world, this Consciousness remains untouched and free of stain.

Just as this energy pervades the universe, it permeates the human body, filling it from head to toe. It is this shakti that carries on all our life functions. It becomes the *prāna* and *apāna,* the incoming and outgoing breaths. It is the power that makes our heart beat and causes the blood to flow in our veins. In this way, this conscious energy powers our bodies.

However, in its inner spiritual aspect, the energy ordinarily lies dormant. The awakening of this latent inner energy is essential for all of us, because only when it is activated and unfolds within us are we truly able to experience the Self.[8] This inner *kundalinī shakti* resides at a subtle energy center known as the *mūlādhāra chakra,* located at the base of the spine. The awakening of this energy is the beginning of a subtle inner process, leading ultimately to the state of union with the Self.

There are several ways this awakening can take place. However, the easiest is through shaktipat, the transmission of energy from a fully Self-realized spiritual Master. In shaktipat, just as a lit candle lights an unlit one, one's inner energy is kindled by the fully unfolded energy of the Guru. Then one no longer has to make an effort to meditate. Meditation comes spontaneously on its own.

KNOWLEDGE

THE UPANISHADS TEACH that we cannot attain the Self simply by doing good actions or by performing rituals. We can attain the Self only through direct knowledge;[9] it is that knowledge which makes us one with God. When our dormant shakti is awakened, this knowledge arises very naturally, and we are able to see the Self.

If we had the right understanding, we could experience God right away. If the sun is out and we go outside, we see it immediately. How much time does it take to see the sun when it is shining in the sky? In the same way, the light of God is shining within us all the time. How long should it take us to perceive that light which shines at every moment in our hearts? This is why the scriptures say that we meditate not to attain God but to perceive the God who is already within us. Kashmir Shaivism says that if one does not already have something, trying to attain it is of no use, since one can lose it in the future. The *Vijñāna Bhairava,* one of the revealed texts of Kashmir Shaivism, teaches that God, the Self, is present in all one's inner feelings, one's inner understanding, and one's inner knowledge.[10] He is closer than anyone or anything; it is only because of our weak understanding that we are not able to know Him.

The sage Vasishtha told Lord Rama, "It is very easy to see God. You can see Him in the time it takes to blink your eyes. Yet many lifetimes have gone by, and you still haven't seen Him."[11]

The Upanishads teach that God is of the form of *sat, chit,* and *ānanda*: absolute Existence, Consciousness, and Bliss. *Sat* means Truth, that which exists in all places, in all things, and at all times. If Truth were not omnipresent, it would not be the Truth; it would not have absolute existence. For example, if you are in New York, you are real in New York, but since you are not in Los Angeles, you are not real there. But God, being sat, is not bound by place or time, nor is He restricted to one particular object. What object is there that is not Shiva?[12] What country is there where Shiva is not? That Consciousness, that God, exists in His fullness in everything. Being present in everything, He is present in our hearts, and we can find Him there.

The next element is *chit. Chit* means Consciousness, or that which illuminates everything. *Chit* is the light of the Self, which destroys ignorance. *Chit* makes us aware of all outer objects, and it also makes us aware that God exists inside. Moreover, if we think that God does not exist because we have not seen Him, it is *chit* that illuminates that understanding. *Chit* is the discloser of the knowledge that something exists or does not exist. *Chit* is that which illuminates all places and all things at all times; therefore, *chit* also illuminates our inner being.

The final element is *ānanda. Ānanda* is absolute bliss, the bliss of Consciousness. This bliss is far superior to the pleasure that arises from seeing a beautiful form, hearing a melodious sound, tasting delicious food, or experiencing the softness of a touch. The pleasure born of looking at a beautiful form depends on that form, and if the form disappears, the bliss also disappears. The pleasure that comes from listening to a melodious sound depends on that sound, and if the sound disappears, the pleasure also disappears. In the same way, the pleasure born of a soft touch depends on that touch, and when the touch is no more, the pleasure also dies. But *ānanda* does not depend on any external factor. It arises, unconditioned, from within. When the mind and intellect come close to the Self, they are able to experience bliss. It is to attain that bliss, to establish ourselves in that bliss, that we meditate. When we attain the light of the Self within ourselves, that light emerges as supreme Love.

So God, the Self, is of the form of *sat, chit, and ānanda.* Being *sat, chit, and ānanda,* He pervades everywhere, and therefore we can see Him anywhere. The real question is, Do we want to see God as He is or as we want Him to be? If we want to see Him as He is, He is manifest; He is not concealed. If the intellect is sufficiently subtle and refined, we can experience Him instantly. This is why the sages agree that, in the attainment of the Self, understanding and knowledge are more important than techniques of meditation. Mere spiritual practice will not help us to know God. People think that by pursuing different practices they can attain Him. They take a course here and do not attain anything; they take a course there and do not attain anything. They take course after course, and the more expensive the course, the more they rush to enroll in it. However, the object of spiritual practice, or sadhana, is not attained by these practices. Kashmir Shaivism speaks of the net of sadhana and says that spiritual practices cannot illuminate the Self any more than a pot can illuminate the sun.[13]

Once Sheikh Nasruddin woke up early in the morning. There was no moon; it was pitch black. He called his disciple Mahmud and asked him to go outside and see if the sun had risen.

Mahmud went out and came back a moment later. "O Nasruddin Sahib, it is very dark outside. I cannot see the sun at all."

"You idiot!" shouted Nasruddin. "Haven't you got the sense to use a flashlight?"

To expect a mere spiritual discipline to illuminate the indwelling God is like trying to see the sun with a flashlight. If the sun has really risen, one does not have to use a flashlight to see it. The flashlight cannot shine beside the sun, nor can darkness bear to remain after the sun has come up. In the same way, no technique can reveal the Self. Nothing can illuminate the Self, because it is the Self that illuminates everything.

It is only because our inner instruments are not refined

enough to approach the Self that we have to meditate.[14] The *Yoga Sūtras* of Patanjali, an authoritative scripture on meditation, explains that although the Self is always blazing within us, the restlessness of the mind acts as a barrier. According to Patanjali, when the mind becomes still and turns inward, we immediately perceive the Self.[15]

THE OBJECT OF MEDITATION

THE FIRST QUESTION THAT ARISES when we sit for meditation is: What should we meditate on? People meditate on all kinds of objects and recommend many different techniques. Maharishi Patanjali speaks of concentration, or *dhāranā,* in which one focuses one's attention on a particular object in order to still and focus the mind.[16] One can concentrate on the heart, on the space between the eyebrows, or on other centers of the body. One can also focus on a being who has risen above passion and attachment; as the mind clings to such a being, it will take on his qualities. In fact, Patanjali says that one may concentrate wherever the mind finds satisfaction.

However, the best object of meditation is the inner Self. When the Self is the goal of meditation, why should we choose another object? If we want to experience the Self, we should meditate on the Self. If we want to know God, we should meditate on God. The mind becomes like that on which it meditates. The poet-saint Sundardas sang:

The mind that always thinks of a woman
takes on a woman's form.
The mind that is always angry
burns in the fire of anger.
The mind that contemplates illusion
falls into the well of illusion.
The mind that continually takes refuge in the Supreme
eventually becomes That.

For this reason, we should choose for the object of meditation that which is our true nature. When we meditate on the Self, not only do we experience the Self, we become the very form of the Self.

Once a seeker asked a sage, "Who is that God on whom I can meditate?" The sage replied, "God is the witness of your mind." That witness is the goal of meditation. The Upanishads say, "It lives in the mind, but the mind cannot know it, because the mind is its body."[17] The Self is the witness of the mind, and it is also the source of the mind. In the *Kena Upanishad*, there is a statement: "That is God who makes the mind think, but who can never be apprehended by the mind."[18] One whom the mind can think about cannot be the supreme Truth, because that Self is the motive power behind all the movements of the mind. The Self makes the mind think, the imagination fantasize, and the ego constantly prattle, "I, I, I." In the same way, God is the one through whose inspiration we meditate.

In the *Gītā*, Lord Krishna says: "O Arjuna, That shines through all our senses yet is without the senses. It supports all the senses yet remains apart from them. It experiences the different qualities of nature yet remains detached from them."[19]

Who is that being who knows all the positive and negative thoughts that come and go in the mind? During meditation, when we have inner problems, that being perceives all of them. That being is of the form of knowledge. It is that which makes us know everything. For example, in meditation, something comes up inside. First we become aware of it; we have the knowledge that it is arising. Then we know exactly what it is. We identify it as a good or bad thought. That which makes us aware of the existence of something and of exactly what it is, is nothing but the Self. It is that pure awareness that is the Self, not our good or bad thoughts. Within and without, whatever action takes place, whatever we do, it is the Self that makes us aware that it is happening. This awareness is constantly there, inside us. It is the pure I-consciousness, without form or attribute. Just as it knows everything inside and outside, it knows itself. To know this knower is true meditation.

HOW TO DEAL WITH THE MIND

THE HIGHEST MEDITATION is the state of complete inner stillness. In that state, not a single thought arises in the mind. However, most people cannot attain this state of stillness right away. For that reason, it is of the greatest importance for a meditator to understand how to deal with the mind.

Most people who meditate make the same mistake. When they sit for meditation, they do not focus on the Self. Instead, they run after the mind, trying to find out what it is doing. People always complain to me, "When I try to meditate, different thoughts keep rushing into my mind." Sometimes their minds are filled with anger, sometimes with hatred, sometimes with lust. At one moment, they are thinking of someone they love; at another moment, they are remembering their past bad actions and are filled with remorse. The more they try to obliterate thoughts from the mind, the more thoughts rush in. Instead of meditating on the Self, they find themselves like the seeker who found himself meditating on a monkey.

Once there was a seeker who went to a Guru to learn meditation. The Guru said, "I will choose an auspicious time for your initiation, and then I will call you." When the auspicious hour came, the Guru called the seeker and made all the proper arrangements for the initiation. After he had completed all the parts of the ritual, he said, "I am going to give you an important instruction. When you sit for meditation, first bow in all four directions and begin to repeat your mantra. But remember one thing. Whatever you do, don't think of a monkey."

"Why on earth would I think of a monkey?" asked the disciple. "I never thought of a monkey in my life. I don't care about monkeys; I care only about God."

When the initiation was over, the young man returned home, spread out a mat, and sat on it, facing east. He took a sip of holy water and bowed in all four directions, and then he began to think about his Guru's last instruction. "What was it my Guru said? Oh, yes, 'Don't think of a monkey.' " Immediately a monkey appeared in his mind.

The seeker was upset. Where did that monkey come from? he wondered. He opened his eyes and took another sip of holy water. Again he recalled what his Guru had said: "Don't think of a monkey." Once again, a monkey stood before him.

The seeker made three, four, five more attempts to meditate and each time was confronted with the monkey. Finally he rushed back to his Guru. "O Guru, O holy seer, what shall I do? Until I came to you, I didn't know what a monkey looked like, and now, when I sit for meditation, a monkey is all I can see."

This is what happens when we try to subdue the mind forcibly in meditation. Instead of worrying about the thoughts in the mind, instead of trying to erase the thoughts from the mind, it would be much better if we tried to understand the nature of the mind. What is the mind? The mind has no independent existence. The Upanishads say that the Self has itself become the mind.[20] The mind is nothing but a contracted form of the supreme Consciousness that has created the universe. The *Pratyabhijñāhridayam* explains this in an aphorism: "Chiti Herself, descending from the plane of pure Consciousness, becomes the mind by contracting in accordance with the object perceived."[21] This means that when Consciousness descends from its status as pure Consciousness and assumes limitations, it becomes the stuff of the mind.

This is easy to understand if we think about what actually comprises the thoughts and images of the mind. The horse, the dog, and the camel that arise in the mind are not made of anything material; they are made of Consciousness. The aphorism says that the mind-stuff that forms itself into a camel, a dog, or a horse is nothing but a pulsation of the same Consciousness that has formed the universe. Another aphorism in the *Pratyabhijñāhridayam* is: "By the power of Her own will alone, She unfolds the universe upon Her own screen,"[22] which means that Consciousness, that divine energy, has created the universe out of its own being, without taking the help of anything outside itself. In the same way, when Consciousness becomes the mind by assuming limitations, it begins to create endless mental universes. There are many outer universes, but they are all contained in Consciousness. In the same way, the universes that vibrate in the mind should not be seen as different from Consciousness. If you can look at your mind in this way, you will have very good meditation.

Let your mind spin as much as it wants to; do not try to subdue it. Simply witness the different thoughts as they arise and subside. No matter what thoughts and images arise in the mind, be aware that there is no concrete material from which they are being manifested. They are simply a phantasmagoria of Consciousness, and no matter how many worlds of desires, wishes, and positive and negative thoughts your mind creates, you should realize that they are all a play of Consciousness. When thoughts or images arise in your meditation, maintain the awareness of equality—the understanding that all objects are nothing but different forms of the Self. Be aware that even the worst thought is God. This understanding is vital to meditation. Your goal is not to battle with the mind, but to witness the mind. Know that you are the witness, the Self, and let the mind go wherever it likes. If you meditate with this awareness—that whatever is, is God—your mind will become calm very soon, and that will be high meditation.

MANTRA

ANOTHER GREAT MEANS of dealing with the mind is to take the support of the mantra. In India, there is a saying that the best way to take a thorn out of one's foot is with another thorn. In the same way, according to the scriptures, when one wants to still the mind, which revels in thoughts, one takes the help of one thought, the mantra.[23]

The word *mantra* means that which redeems and protects the one who contemplates it. Mantra is the very life of meditation, the greatest of all techniques. A mantra is a cosmic word or sound vibration. It is the vibration of the Self, the true speech of the Self, and when we immerse ourselves in it, it leads us to the place of the Self.

Mantras consist of letters, which form words, which form sentences, which take us to their goal. Whether in mundane or spiritual life, all our work is carried out through mantras, through words. Without words, we cannot communicate with one another.

Mantras bear their fruit very quickly. The great saint Tukaram said: "When the name of God is on the tongue, liberation is in your hand." This should not be surprising, because in mundane life we use words, and they bear fruit immediately. I can make you happy immediately by using a few sweet words, by praising you and saying how beautiful you are. I can also make you agitated by using a few abusive words, by saying how bad you are.

Once a saint was giving a lecture on mantra. He was saying, "Mantra is great. Mantra takes us to God." Someone shouted from the back of the room, "How can you say that a mantra takes us to God? If I say, 'Bread, bread, bread,' will that get me bread?"

"Sit down, you bastard!" the saint shouted.

When the man heard this, he became furious. He began to shake and his hair stood on end. Even his necktie began to vibrate. He shouted, "You call yourself a saint, and yet you use such a filthy word for me?"

"I'm sorry, sir," the saint said. "Please, be calm and tell me what happened."

"You have the audacity to ask me what happened! Don't you realize how you have insulted me?"

"I used just one abusive word," the saint said, "and it has had such a powerful effect on you! When this is the case with an abusive term, what makes you think that the name of God, which is the supreme Truth, does not have its own power and will not also affect you?" If abusive words can make our blood boil, how can the name of God not have the power to change us?

Mantra has the greatest power. The sages of India, through the power of mantra, could burn whole mountains without fire. Through the power of mantra, they could bring entire universes into existence.

The scriptures say, *mantra maheshvara,* "Mantra is God." There is no difference between God and His name; mantra has all the power of God. In the Gītā, the Lord says: *mantro'ham,* "[In all rituals] I am the mantra."[24] As we repeat the mantra, we should focus our attention within, on the place that is the source of the mantra. As we repeat the mantra more and more, it penetrates the entire territory of our mind, our intellect, and our imagination, and purifies it completely.

It is very important to repeat the mantra with the understanding of its meaning. Moreover, one who wants to attain the power of mantra, who wants to merge in mantra, should have the awareness that the goal of the mantra is one's own Self, that there is no difference between oneself, the mantra, and the goal of the mantra. If we hear an abusive word, we immediately identify ourselves as the object of that word, and that is why it has such an effect on us.

The only reason that a mantra does not affect us as profoundly as an abusive word is that we do not identify with it in the same way. If a person keeps himself, the mantra, and the goal of the mantra separate, he will never realize the goal of the mantra. Kashmir Shaivism says that we should meditate on God by becoming God; only then can we attain God.[25]

There are eighty-four million mantras that can be found in books or obtained from different teachers. However, a mantra is not truly effective unless it is a conscious mantra, an alive mantra. A conscious mantra is one that has been received from a Guru who received it from his own Guru, repeated it himself, and attained full realization of his own inner Self. Such a mantra has the full power of the Guru's realization behind it, and when we repeat it in meditation, our meditation becomes infused with the force of that realization.

The power that flows through such a Self-realized Guru is the grace-bestowing power of the Supreme, and that same power exists in his mantra. Traditionally, a Guru initiates a disciple through a mantra, and mantra is one of the means through which the Guru gives shaktipat. As we repeat it with great love and reverence during meditation, it begins to work within. The energy of the Guru's conscious mantra, which is the energy of the supreme Guru, enters us and awakens our own inner energy, our own shakti.

ĀSANA

ANOTHER IMPORTANT FACTOR in meditation is the sitting posture, or *āsana*. The sitting posture is the foundation on which the whole structure of yoga rests. The *Yoga Sūtras* say that the correct sitting posture is that in which one can sit comfortably for a long time.[26] For meditation, the most important thing in *āsana* is that the spine be kept straight. If the back is kept straight, the mind becomes steady in the heart.

There are three sitting postures that are suitable for meditation; however, if one is too uncomfortable sitting, one can stretch out on the back in *shavāsana,* the corpse pose, and meditate in that position. The three main postures are *padmāsana,* the lotus posture; *siddhāsana,* the perfect posture;

and *sukhāsana,* the easy posture. Everyone must be familiar with the lotus posture, in which the legs are folded one over the other. The lotus is particularly important because if one sits in this position for one and one-half hours, it will completely purify the seventy-two million *nādīs,* or inner subtle channels. If you cannot sit in the lotus posture, sit in the easy posture, with one leg folded over the other. If you keep sitting in either of these postures steadily, the mind will begin to turn inward, and meditation will happen on its own. When you keep moving the body continually, the mind becomes restless. As the posture becomes steady, the *prāna* automatically becomes steady. As the *prāna* becomes steady, the mind becomes steady, and as the mind becomes steady, you begin to drink the joy that is in the heart.

PRĀNĀYĀMA

THE FINAL FACTOR IN MEDITATION is *prānāyāma,* the breathing process. People practice many different kinds of *prānāyāma.* Some people practice it so much that they ruin their minds, their intellects, and their bodies. In meditation, the breathing process should be natural and spontaneous. We should not try to disturb the natural rhythm of the breath.

The mind and the *prāna* work in conjunction with each other. So let the rhythm of your breathing be natural. As you repeat the mantra, the breath will go in and out in time with the rhythm of the mantra and will become steady by itself.

THE PROCESS OF MEDITATION

THERE ARE FOUR FACTORS INVOLVED in meditation: the object of meditation, which is the inner Self; mantra, which is the vibration of the Self; *āsana,* the posture in which we can sit comfortably for a long time; and natural *prāṇāyāma,* which arises when we repeat the mantra with love and reverence. These four factors are interrelated, and when they come together, meditation occurs in a very natural manner.

Meditation on the Self is very easy. All that we really need are love and interest. As we meditate more and more, the inner shakti awakens and begins to unfold. The more intensely we long for meditation, the more we long for God, the more desire we have for the inner awakening, the closer we come to it. And the more we honor the shakti, the more we revere and worship it, the more actively it works inside us. When three factors come together—our faith in the shakti, the shakti, and the Guru, who is the activator of the shakti—there is an explosion of meditation within. Just as the shakti creates universes in the outer world, when it begins to work inside us, it creates a new inner universe, a universe of unending enthusiasm, a universe of supreme bliss.

The inner universe is much greater than the outer universe; it is so vast that the entire outer cosmos can be kept in just one corner of it. Everything is contained within it, and that is why, in meditation, the Indian seers were able to discover all the secrets of the universe.

Within us are infinite miracles, infinite wonders. As we go deeper into meditation, we come to understand the reality of all the different inner worlds we read about in the scriptures. Within these inner spaces, nectarean music resounds—all the different musical instruments were originally made by yogis after they had listened to this inner music. Within us are such delicious nectars that nothing in this world can compare with them in sweetness. There are suns so effulgent that the outer sun looks dull beside them. We should meditate systematically and with great persistence and go deeper and deeper within the body. In this way, meditation will be a gradual unfolding of our inner being.

Along the way will be many experiences, and these experiences are fine. However, the true state is beyond them. As we go deeper into meditation, we reach a place where we see nothing and hear nothing. Here there is nothing but bliss. This is the place of the Self, and true meditation is to become immersed in That.[27]

The seers of Vedanta explained that our spirit is encased not just in one body, but in four, and that as we meditate we pass through each of these four bodies to the Truth that lies within them.[28] The first is the physical body, in which we experience the waking state. This is the state in which we identify ourselves as the body. When we are in the waking state, if the body is experiencing pain and pleasure, we say, "I am experiencing pain," or "I am experiencing pleasure." As the shakti begins to work in this body, we may experience physical movements, called *kriyās,* that are part of the process of purification of the physical body. In meditation, when the meditator is in the gross state, he can see the physical body as a red light that surrounds him like a flame of fire. This light is the size of the body, and within it one can see many marvelous things. Sometimes one can even see the vital force and the different fluids circulating within the body.

As meditation deepens, the meditator passes from the gross body to the subtle body, which one can see as a white light. This light dwells in the throat center and is the size of the thumb. One experiences dreams in the subtle body; in this state, one becomes aware that one is different from the physical body.

As the meditator goes deeper, he passes from the white, thumb-sized light to the light of the third body, which is black and the size of a fingertip. This is the causal body, the body of deep sleep. It is the state of total darkness, of total oblivion. In this state, the small self retires into the universal Self, and one is not even conscious of who or what one is. In this state, one experiences great peace. This is the state of the void.

However, if a seeker has deep love for the Guru and has deep faith in his grace and in the *kundalinī*, he passes from the third plane to the fourth plane, the state of turīya, the transcendent state. Then he sees the tiny blue light, the light of the Self, which we call the Blue Pearl.

The Blue Pearl is the most intimate body of the soul, and it is fascinatingly beautiful. As meditation deepens, one begins to see it sparkling and scintillating in the topmost spiritual center, the *sahasrāra*. The Blue Pearl is the vehicle of the individual soul. It is in the Blue Pearl that the soul leaves the body after death and travels to different worlds. It is extremely fine and subtle, and it moves like lightning. Sometimes it comes out of the meditator's eyes and stands in front of him, moving so subtly that the eyes do not feel its passage.

The Blue Pearl is the size of a sesame seed, but in reality it is so vast that it contains the entire universe.[29] We are able to function because of the dynamism of the Blue Pearl. Because of its presence, the breath moves in and out of our bodies. The rays of its divine love keep flowing through us, and because of these rays we feel love for each other. The light of the Blue Pearl lights up our faces and our hearts; it is because of this light that we give love to others. If this light left the body, the body would have no radiance and no attraction. It would be of no use to anyone, and it would have to be discarded. The Blue Pearl is the abode of God, the form of the Self within us. Once you begin to see it in yourself, you will also begin to see it in others. As you continue to meditate, one day this light will expand, and within it you will see the entire cosmos. As you become immersed in this light, you will know, "I am God. I am Brahman." It was after having this experience that the Sufi saint Mansur Mastana said, "Whatever I see around me is nothing but an expansion of my own being. I am not this body. I am the light that spreads everywhere."

This state is the culmination of meditation. In this state, our limitations vanish; our sense of individuality melts away. We attain divine vision, so that we no longer see this world as filled with duality and diversity. Instead of seeing differences between man and woman, East and West, past and future, we understand this whole universe as an expansion of our own Self. We realize that everything is a play of Consciousness and that, just as the bubbles and waves of the ocean arise and subside in the ocean, whatever exists arises and subsides in the Self.

It is to attain this state that one should meditate, that one's shakti should be awakened. After one has reached this state, one no longer has to close one's eyes and sit for meditation; meditation goes on all the time. During formal meditation one experiences the highest bliss, but even in the waking state one experiences the joy of *samādhi,* seeing the entire waking world as an expansion of the same Consciousness. Wherever one looks, one sees God. Whatever one hears, one hears God. This is known as the state of natural *samādhi,* the state of the great beings, and in this state one continuously drinks the bliss that is in the heart.

SIDDHA MEDITATION

IF WE ARE GOING TO REALIZE this state of oneness at the end of our practice of meditation, why should we not understand it at the beginning and practice meditation with the awareness that everything is Shiva? This is how the great beings meditate, and if we also learn to see with this awareness, our meditation will be great. To meditate in this way, we do not have to undergo any difficulties. We do not have to make the mind still. We do not even have to close our eyes. Utpaladeva, the great sage and philosopher of Kashmir Shaivism, says: "One who is constantly aware that this entire universe is his own glory retains his divinity even if thoughts and fancies play in his mind."[30]

Truly speaking, everything is Consciousness. It is only because of our sense of limited individuality that we see things differently. A man is Consciousness, a woman is Consciousness, a dog is Consciousness, a donkey is Consciousness, a stone is Consciousness, and a mountain is Consciousness. This is true understanding. This is the knowledge we obtain through meditation, and the moment we obtain this knowledge, we begin to understand everything as it is.

In order to rid yourself of the feeling of limitation and obtain this understanding, you should practice the sadhana of Shiva. You should understand, "I am Shiva—God. It is God who is meditating, and all the objects of my meditation are God. My sadhana is God, and everybody and everything I see is God." For a long time, you have had the awareness, "I am an individual being, I am small, I am limited." This is why it is difficult for you to accept immediately the awareness, "I am God." All your life, you have been hearing that you are a sinner. Your teachers, all the holy books, and people pursuing different religious paths have been telling you that you are a sinner, and you have come to believe it. In this way, you impose the idea of sin onto the Self, which is totally pure and free of sin. It is because one has this wrong understanding that one identifies oneself with the wrong things. That is why one cannot uplift oneself; that is why one cannot have faith in the Self or become one-pointed on the Self. Kashmir Shaivism teaches that when one begins to think, "I am this, I am that, I am a sinner, I am an inferior person," one becomes poor in shakti, and that is how one becomes an individual being.

In Vedanta, this is often explained by a story. One day, a washerman took several donkeys to a forest to graze them. There he came upon a lion cub; he did not know that it was a lion, and he brought it home with him. The lion cub grew up with the donkeys. Living in their company, he began to repeat the donkey mantra, *hee-haw, hee-haw,* to eat with them, and to travel back and forth to the river carrying filthy laundry. As the lion grew up, he thought of himself as a donkey and shared the donkeys' habits and their ways.

One day when he was grazing on the river bank with his donkey brothers, another lion came along to drink from the river. While this lion was drinking, he suddenly caught sight of the young lion in the midst of the donkeys. The old lion was shocked to see his brother in such a pitiful condition. He moved closer to him and said, "Brother, what are you up to?"

"I am with my brothers," said the young lion.

"How can you call them brothers? They are asses and you are a lion. Come with me and look at your reflection in the water. Look at your reflection and my reflection, and see if there is anything similar about us."

The young lion gazed down at his reflection and saw that he looked just like the old lion.

"Are they your brothers or am I your brother? Now stop going *hee-haw* and start roaring!"

The young lion began to roar, and all the donkeys ran

away. The two lions ran into the forest. The young lion had been transformed from a donkey to a lion; he had become free.

Actually, the lion cub had never been a donkey. He had only thought he was a donkey, and this is exactly the situation we are in. We are not donkeys. We are not limited, imperfect beings. We are not sinners. We never became small; we only believe we are small. So we must discard this belief and become aware of our own strength. Kashmir Shaivism says that when *chiti*, universal Consciousness, accepts limitations, it begins to believe itself to be bound.[31] Just as *chiti* becomes smaller and smaller by descending from its status as pure Consciousness and becomes a limited individual soul, when it reverses the process, it can become greater and greater and regain its original nature. It is only our awareness that has to be changed. We never became donkeys and we never can become donkeys because we are the pure Self.

To rid yourself of wrong understanding, you do not have to do anything new. All you have to do is meditate. The fact is that you meditate not to attain God, but to become aware that God is within you. Kashmir Shaivism says: "*Nāshivam vidyate kvachit,* Nothing exists that is not Shiva."[32] Where is that place where there is no Shiva? Where is that time where there is no Shiva? So even if you experience duality, even if you see diversity around you, consider yourself to be Shiva. Understand that it is Shiva who is eating, Shiva who is the food that is eaten, Shiva who gives, and Shiva who takes. It is Shiva who does everything. The entire universe is the glory of Shiva, the glory of the Self.

MEDITATION INSTRUCTIONS

Preparing for Meditation

IT IS VERY GOOD TO SET ASIDE a place for meditation. If possible, have a special room, but if not, a corner will do. Purify it by chanting God's name, and try not to let anything take place there that will disturb its atmosphere. In the place where you meditate regularly, the vibrations of meditation gather, and after a while it becomes very easy to meditate there. For the same reason, you should set aside special clothes and a mat for meditation; do not wash them too often, because the shakti will accumulate in them and make it easy for you to meditate.

If possible, meditate at the same time every day. The early hours of the morning, between three and six, are the best for meditation, but you can meditate at any time that is convenient. If you become accustomed to meditating at a certain hour, your body will develop the habit of meditation. I have been meditating every morning at three o'clock for many years, and even now my body automatically goes into meditation at that hour.

The Attitude of Meditation

JUST AS YOU SLIP EASILY into sleep, you should be able to slip easily into meditation. Sit peacefully; be with yourself. Focus your mind on the inner Consciousness, the inner knower. Let your breath move naturally and watch it; do not force anything. Become immersed in your own inner Self. Turn your mind and senses inward. Absorb yourself in the pure "I."

If thoughts arise, let them come and go. Watch the source of your thoughts. Meditate with the awareness that you are the witness of the mind. True meditation is to become free from mentation. The moment the thoughts become still, the light of the Self will shine from within. However, if the mind does not immediately become thought-free, do not try to erase the thoughts forcibly. Respect the mind, understanding that whatever comes and goes within it is a form of the Self. Then it will become still on its own.

To help in stilling the mind, you may take the support of the mantra. Repeat either *Om Namah Shivāya* or *So'ham*. Both mantras are one; both come from the Self. Only the method of repeating them differs.

Om Namah Shivāya

OM NAMAH SHIVĀYA MEANS, "I bow to the Lord, who is the inner Self." Repeat it silently, at the same rate of speed with which you speak. Repeat it with love, and go deep inside. Understand that you yourself are the deity of the mantra. Listen to it. When every letter pulsates in your mind, try to experience it.

Lose yourself in meditation. No matter what feeling arises, let it be. Do not fear. The inner energy is filled with infinite techniques, processes, and feelings. Its play is in everything. Therefore, everything belongs to it, and it is one with your Self.

The purpose of meditation is inner happiness, inner peace. It is fine to have visions, but they are not absolutely necessary. What is necessary is inner joy. When all the senses become quiet and you experience bliss, that is the attainment. The world is the embodiment of joy; joy lies everywhere. Find it and attain it. Instead of having negative thoughts, have the awareness, "I am pure, I am joy." Feel good about yourself; fill yourself with great divinity.

Meditate with this understanding: "Neither am I different from God, nor is God different from me." Then not only will you attain God, but you yourself will become God.

Become quiet with the awareness that everything is you and you are everything.

Meditate on your Self. Honor your Self. Understand your Self. God dwells within you as you.

Your own,

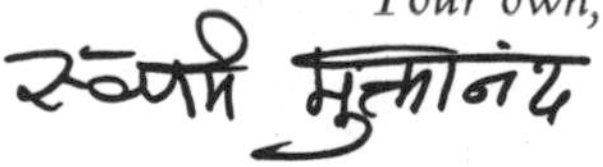

SWAMI MUKTANANDA

Guide to Sanskrit Pronunciation

For the reader's convenience, the Sanskrit and Hindi terms most frequently used in Siddha Yoga literature and courses appear throughout the text in roman type with simple transliteration. *Śaktipāta,* for instance, is shaktipat; *sādhanā* is sadhana, and so on. For less frequently used Sanskrit words, the long vowels are marked in the text. The standard international transliteration for each Sanskrit term is given in the notes and in brackets for the glossary entries.

For readers not familiar with Sanskrit, the following is a guide for pronunciation.

Vowels

Sanskrit vowels are categorized as either long or short. In English transliteration, the long vowels are marked with a bar above the letter and are pronounced twice as long as the short vowels. *E, ai, au,* and *o* are always pronounced as long vowels.

Short:	Long:	
a as in c*u*p	*ā* as in c*a*lm	*ai* as in *ai*sle
i as in g*i*ve	*e* as in s*a*ve	*au* as in c*ow*
u as in f*u*ll	*ī* as in s*ee*n	*ū* as in sch*oo*l
	o as in kn*ow*	

Consonants

The main differences between Sanskrit and English pronunciation of consonants are in the aspirated and retroflexive letters.

The aspirated letters have *a* definite *h* sound. The Sanskrit letter *kh* is pronounced as in in*kh*orn; the *th* as in boa*th*ouse; the *ph* as in loo*ph*ole.

The retroflexes are pronounced with the tip of the tongue touching the hard palate; *ṭ,* for instance, is pronounced as in an*t*; *ḍ* as in en*d*.

The sibilants are *ś, ṣ,* and *s*. The *ś* is pronounced as *sh* but with the tongue touching the soft palate; the *ṣ* as *sh* with the tongue touching the hard palate; the *s* as in hi*s*tory.

Other distinctive consonants are these:

c as in *ch*urch	*ṃ* is a strong nasal
ch as in pit*ch-h*ook	*ḥ* is a strong aspiration
ñ as in ca*ny*on	*ṛ* as in w*ri*tten

For a detailed pronunciation guide, see
The Nectar of Chanting, published by Chitshakti Publications.

Notes

1. *Bhagavadgītā*, 13.2.
   idaṃ śarīraṃ kāunteya kṣetram ity abhidhīyate /
   etad yo vetti taṃ prāhuḥ kṣetrajña iti tadvidaḥ //
2. *Bhagavadgītā*, 13.3.
   kṣetrajñaṃ cāpi māṃ viddhi sarvakṣetreṣu bhārata
3. *Ātmabodha*, 36.
4. See *Chāndogyopaniṣad*, 7.6.1.
5. See *Ātmabodha*, 22: "Attachment, desire, pleasure, pain are perceived to exist only as long as the mind functions. . . . Therefore, they belong to the mind alone and not to the Self."
6. *Bṛhajjābālopaniṣad*, 8.6.
7. Kshemaraja, *Pratyabhijñāhṛdayam*, 1.
   citiḥ svatantrā viśvasiddhihetuḥ
8. For further information about *kundalinī*, see Swami Muktananda, *Kundalini: The Secret of Life* and *Play of Consciousness*; see also Swami Kripananda, *The Sacred Power*; all published by Chitshakti Publications.
9. Knowledge refers here to the direct perceptual experience in which the Self is "seen" illuminating itself, without the aid of the senses, mind, or intellect.
10. See *Vijñānabhairava*, 98: *icchāyām athavā jñāne jāte cittaṃ niveśayet / ātmabuddhyananyacetas tatas tattvārthadarśanam //*
    "When a desire or knowledge or activity appears, one should, with the mind withdrawn from all objects [of desire, knowledge, etc.], fix the mind on the desire, . . . understanding it as the Self. Then one will have the realization of the essential Reality."
11. *Yoga Vāsiṣṭha*.
12. Shiva, in this connection, refers not to the Hindu deity, but to the all-pervasive Consciousness, or God, of which Shiva is one name.
13. See Abhinavagupta, *Tantrasāra*: "The net of sadhana cannot reveal Shiva. Can a clay pot illuminate the conscious sun?"
14. Although the Self is self-luminous and does not depend on any outside agency to be experienced, the intellect, mind, and other instruments serve as vehicles through which the Self is approached. Therefore, Self-realization cannot take place unless they are refined and purified.
15. See Patanjali, *Yogasūtra*, 1.2: *yogaś citta-vṛtti-nidrodhaḥ*, "Yoga is to still the ripples

of the mind"; and I.3: *tadā draṣṭuḥ svarūpe 'vasthānam*, "Then the seer is estab lished in his own essential nature."

16. *Yogasūtra*, 3.1.

17. *Bṛhadāraṇyakopaniṣad*, 3.7.20.

18. *Kenopaniṣad*, 1.5.

19. *Bhagavadgītā*, 13.15.
sarvendriyaguṇābhāsaṃ sarvendriyavivarjitam /
asaktaṃ sarvabhṛc cāiva nirguṇaṃ guṇabhoktṛ ca //

20. *Muṇḍakopaniṣad*, 2.1.3: "From Him are born life, mind, all the sense organs. . . ."

21. *Pratyabhijñāhṛdayam*, 5.
citireva cetanapadādavarūḍhācetyasaṅkocinī cittam

22. *Pratyabhijñāhṛdayam*, 2.
svecchayā svabittau viśvam unmīlayati

23. See *Yogasūtra*, 1.27-29. According to Vyasa, an early commentator on the *Yogasūtra*, "The repetition of mantra and contemplation of its goal allow the mind to become concentrated."

24. *Bhagavadgītā*, 9.16.

25. See Somananda, *Śiva Dṛṣṭi*:
śivo 'smi sādhanāviṣṭaḥ śivo 'haṃ yājako 'pyaham /
śivaṃ yāmi śivo yāmi śivena śiva sādhanaḥ //
"Practice sadhana with the following awareness: I am a form of Shiva. I will attain Shiva. By becoming Him, I will attain Him. Because I am Shiva, I will attain Shivahood very easily. This is the sadhana to attain Shiva."

26. *Yogasūtra*, 2.46.

27. In this state, the mind and senses are stilled, yet there is total awareness. See Swami Muktananda, *Play of Consciousness*, "Final Realization."

28. For a more detailed description of meditation in the four bodies, see Swami Muktananda, *Play of Consciousness*.

29. Tukaram Maharaj, the seventeenth-century Maharashtrian poet-saint, says in one of his verses: "God, the nourisher of the universe, has made his dwelling place in a house as small as a sesame seed."

30. *Īśvarapratyabhijñā*, 4.1.12.
sarvo mamāyaṃ vibhava ityevaṃ parijānataḥ /
viśvātmano vikalpanaṃ prasre 'pi maheśatā //

31. *Pratyabhijñāhṛdayam*, 9: *cidvat tacchakti-saṅkocāt malāvṛtaḥ saṃsārī*
"Because of contraction, universal Consciousness becomes an ordinary being, subject to limitations."

32. *Svacchandatantra*. Quoted in Swami Muktananda, *Nothing Exists That Is Not Śiva*, p. 72.

Glossary

ABSOLUTE, THE
The highest Reality; supreme Consciousness; the pure, untainted, changeless Truth.

AHAM BRAHMASMI
[*ahaṃ brahmāsmi*]
One of the four great statements (*mahāvākyas*) of Vedanta. It means, "I am Brahman," the supreme Absolute. *See also* VEDANTA.

APANA [*apāna*]
Inhalation, one of the five types of *prāna*; the downward-moving energy that controls the abdomen and excretion of wastes from the body. *See also* PRANA.

ARJUNA
One of the warrior heroes from the *Mahābhārata* epic; a great disciple of Lord Krishna. It was to Arjuna that Krishna imparted his teaching in the *Bhagavad Gītā*. *See also* BHAGAVAD GITA; KRISHNA.

ASANA [*āsana*]
1) A hatha yoga posture practiced to strengthen and purify the body and develop one-pointedness of mind. 2) A seat or mat on which one sits for meditation.

ASHRAM [*āśrama*]
The dwelling place of a Guru or saint; a monastic retreat site where seekers engage in spiritual practices and study the sacred teachings of yoga.

BHAGAVAD GITA [*bhagavadgītā*]
(*lit.*, The Song of the Lord) One of the world's greatest works of spiritual literature, part of the epic *Mahābhārata*. In the *Gītā*, Lord Krishna explains the path of liberation to Arjuna on the battlefield. *See also* ARJUNA; KRISHNA.

BHAGAWAN [*bhagavān*]
(*lit.*, the Lord) One who is glorious, illustrious, and venerable. A term of great honor. Baba Muktananda's Guru is known as Bhagawan Nityananda. *See also* NITYANANDA, BHAGAWAN.

BISTAMI, HAZRIT BAYAZID
(777-848) An ecstatic Sufi saint of northeastern Persia; author of many poems that boldly portray the mystic's total absorption in God. Also known as Abu Yazid al-Bistami.

BLUE PEARL
(Sanskrit: *nīla bindu*) A brilliant blue light, the size of a tiny seed, that appears to the meditator whose *kundalinī* energy has been awakened; it is the subtle abode of the inner Self.

BRAHMAN [*brahman*]
In Vedic philosophy, the absolute Reality or all-pervasive supreme Principle of the universe.

BRIHAJJABALA UPANISHAD
[*bṛhajjābālopaniṣad*]
From the *Atharva Veda*, this minor Upanishad is an exposition of the

divinity of Kalagni Rudra, a form of Lord Shiva. *See also* UPANISHADS.

CHAKRA [*cakra*]
(*lit.*, wheel) An energy center located in the subtle body. There are seven major chakras. When the *kundalinī* energy is awakened, it flows upward from the *mūlādhāra chakra* at the base of the spine to the *sahasrāra* at the crown of the head. *See also* KUNDALINI.

CHIDVILASANANDA, SWAMI
(*lit.*, the bliss of the play of Consciousness) The name given to Gurumayi by her Guru, Swami Muktananda, when she took the vows of monkhood in 1982.

CHITI [*citi*]
Divine conscious energy; the creative aspect of God. *See also* KUNDALINI; SHAKTI.

CONSCIOUSNESS
The intelligent, supremely independent, divine energy that creates, pervades, and supports the entire universe. *See also* CHITI; SHAKTI.

DHARANA [*dhāraṇā*]
The yogic practice of concentration in which the mind becomes stabilized by being fixed on an object; a spiritual exercise that leads one to the experience of God within.

EGO
In yoga, the limited sense of "I" that is identified with the body, mind, and senses; sometimes described as "the veil of suffering."

GANESHPURI
A village at the foot of Mandagni Mountain in Maharashtra, India. Bhagawan Nityananda settled in this region, where yogis have performed spiritual practices for thousands of years. The ashram founded by Swami Muktananda at his Guru's command is built on this sacred land. *See also* GURUDEV SIDDHA PEETH.

GURU [*guru*]
A spiritual Master who has attained oneness with God and who is able both to initiate seekers and to guide them on the spiritual path to liberation. A Guru is also required to be learned in the scriptures and must belong to a lineage of Masters. *See also* SHAKTIPAT; SIDDHA.

GURUDEV SIDDHA PEETH
(*lit.*, abode of the Siddhas) The main Siddha Yoga ashram, located in Ganeshpuri, India; the site of the Samadhi Shrine of Swami Muktananda. *See also* ASHRAM; GANESHPURI.

GURUMAYI
A term of respect and endearment often used in addressing Swami Chidvilasananda.

HATHA YOGA [*haṭhayoga*]
Yogic practices, both physical and mental, performed for the purpose of purifying and strengthening the physical and subtle bodies. *See also* YOGA.

KASHMIR SHAIVISM
A branch of the Shaivite philosophical tradition, propounded by Kashmiri sages, that explains how the formless supreme Principle, Shiva, manifests as the universe. Together with Vedanta,

Kashmir Shaivism provides the basic scriptural context for Siddha Yoga meditation.

KENA UPANISHAD [*kenopaniṣad*]
A principal Upanishad; it establishes that Brahman is the supreme Reality by whom the mind, speech, and senses perform their functions. *See also* UPANISHADS.

KRISHNA [*kṛṣṇa*]
(*lit.*, dark one) The eighth incarnation of Lord Vishnu. The spiritual teachings of Lord Krishna to his disciple Arjuna are contained in the *Bhagavadgītā*. *See also* ARJUNA; BHAGAVAD GITA.

KRIYA [*kriyā*]
A physical, mental, or emotional movement initiated by the awakened *kundalinī* to prepare one for higher states of meditation.

KUNDALINI [*kuṇḍalinī*]
(*lit.*, coiled one) The supreme power, primordial shakti, or energy that lies coiled at the base of the spine in each person. Through the descent of grace (shaktipat), this extremely subtle force is awakened and begins to purify the entire being, traveling upward through the central channel (*sushumnā nādī*), piercing the various subtle energy centers (chakras), and finally reaching the *sahasrāra* at the crown of the head. There, the individual self merges into the supreme Self, and the cycle of birth and death comes to an end. *See also* CHAKRA; SHAKTIPAT.

LIBERATION
Freedom from the cycle of birth and death; the state of realization of oneness with the Absolute.

MAHASAMADHI [*mahāsamādhi*]
(*lit.*, the great union) A realized yogi's conscious departure from the body at death. *See also* SAMADHI.

MANSUR MASTANA
(852-922) An ecstatic Sufi poet-saint who lived most of his life in Baghdad. He was hanged as a heretic for his pronouncement: *Ana'l-haqq*, "I am God," which orthodox Muslims of those days would not tolerate.

MANTRA [*mantra*]
(*lit.*, sacred invocation) The names of God; sacred words or divine sounds invested with the power to protect, purify, and transform the individual who repeats them. A mantra received from an enlightened Master is filled with the power of the Master's attainment. *See also* OM NAMAH SHIVAYA; SO'HAM.

NASRUDDIN, SHEIKH
A figure originating in Turkish folklore during the Middle Ages. He is traditionally used by spiritual teachers to illustrate the antics of the human mind.

NITYANANDA, BHAGAWAN
(d.1961) A great Siddha Master, Swami Muktananda's Guru, also known as Bade Baba ("elder" Baba). He was a born Siddha, living his entire life in the highest state of consciousness. In both Gurudev Siddha Peeth in Ganeshpuri, India, and Shree Muktananda Ashram in South Fallsburg,

New York, Swami Muktananda has dedicated a temple of meditation to honor Bhagawan Nityananda.

OM [*oṃ*]
The primal sound from which the universe emanates; the inner essence of all mantras.

OM NAMAH SHIVAYA
[*oṃ namaḥ śivāya*]
(*lit.*, Om, salutations to Shiva) The Sanskrit mantra of the Siddha Yoga lineage; known as the great redeeming mantra because of its power to grant both worldly fulfillment and spiritual realization. Here Shiva denotes the inner Self.

PATANJALI
A fourth-century sage and the author of the famous *Yoga Sūtras*, the exposition of one of the six orthodox philosophies of India and the authoritative text of the path of meditation.

PRANA [*prāṇa*]
The vital, life-sustaining force of both the individual body and the entire universe.

PRANAYAMA [*prāṇāyāma*]
(*lit.*, restraining the breath) A yogic technique, consisting of systematic regulation and restraint of the breath, that leads to steadiness of mind.

PRATYABHIJNAHRIDAYAM
[*pratyabhijñāhṛdayam*]
(*lit.*, the heart of the doctrine of recognition) An eleventh-century treatise by Kshemaraja that summarizes the *pratyabhijñā* philosophy of Kashmir Shaivism. It states, in essence, that individuals have forgotten their true nature by identifying with the body, and that realization is a process of recognizing or remembering one's true nature (*pratyabhijñā*), which is the inner Self of supreme bliss and love.

RAMA [*rāma*]
(*lit.*, one who is pleasing, delightful) The seventh incarnation of Lord Vishnu, Rama is seen as the embodiment of righteousness and is the object of great devotion. He is the central character in the Indian epic *Rāmāyana.*

SADHANA [*sādhanā*]
1) A spiritual discipline or path. 2) Practices, both physical and mental, on the spiritual path.

SAHASRARA [*sahasrāra*]
The thousand-petaled spiritual energy center at the crown of the head, where one experiences the highest states of consciousness. *See also* CHAKRA; KUNDALINI.

SAMADHI [*samādhi*]
The state of meditative union with the Absolute. *See also* MAHASAMADHI.

SELF
Divine Consciousness residing in the individual, described as the witness of the mind, or the pure I-awareness.

SHAKTI [*Śakti*]
Spiritual power; the divine cosmic power that, according to Shaivite philosophy, creates and maintains the universe. The immanent aspect of divine Consciousness. *See also* CHITI; KUNDALINI.

SHAKTIPAT [*Śaktipāta*]
(*lit.*, descent of grace) Yogic initiation in which the Siddha Guru transmits spiritual energy into the aspirant, thereby awakening the aspirant's dormant *kundalinī*. *See also* GURU; KUNDALINI; SHAKTI.

SHANKARACHARYA
(788-820) A venerated sage who spread the philosophy of Advaita Vedanta, absolute nondualism, throughout India, establishing monastic orders that exist to this day. Among his many works is the *Viveka Chūdāmani*, "The Crest Jewel of Discrimination."

SHIVA [*Śiva*]
1) A name for the one supreme Reality. 2) One of the Hindu trinity of gods, representing God as the destroyer, often understood by yogis as the destroyer of barriers to one's identification with the supreme Self.

SHIVA SUTRAS [*śivasūtra*]
A Sanskrit text revealed by Lord Shiva to the ninth-century sage Vasuguptacharya. It consists of seventy-seven *sūtras*, or aphorisms, that, according to tradition, were found inscribed on a rock in Kashmir. The *Shiva Sūtras* are the scriptural authority for the philosophical school known as Kashmir Shaivism. *See also* KASHMIR SHAIVISM.

SIDDHA [*siddha*]
An enlightened yogi; one who lives in the state of unity-consciousness; one whose experience of the supreme Self is uninterrupted and whose identification with the ego has been dissolved.

SIDDHA YOGA [*siddhayoga*]
(*lit.*, the yoga of perfection) A path to union of the individual and the Divine that begins with shaktipat, the inner awakening by the grace of a Siddha Guru. *Siddha Yoga* is the name Swami Muktananda gave to this path, which he first brought to the West in 1970; Gurumayi Chidvilasananda is the living Master of this lineage. *See also* GURU; KUNDALINI; SHAKTIPAT.

SO'HAM [*so'ham*]
(*lit.*, I am That) *So'ham* is the mantra that describes the natural vibration of the Self, which occurs spontaneously with each incoming and outgoing breath. By becoming aware of *So'ham*, a seeker experiences the identity of the individual self with the supreme Self. Also repeated as *Hamsa*.

SUNDARDAS
(1596-1689) A poet-saint who lived in Delhi and wrote eloquently about the significance of the spiritual Master and the requirements of discipleship. The main collection of his *bhajans*, devotional songs, is the *Sundar Granthavāti*.

TUKARAM MAHARAJ
(1608-1650) A poet-saint who was a grocer in the village of Dehu in Maharashtra. He received initiation in a dream. Tukaram wrote thousands of devotional songs, many of which describe his spiritual experiences and the glory of the divine Name.

TURIYA [*turīya*]
The fourth or transcendental state, beyond the waking, dream, and deep-sleep states, in which the true nature

of reality is directly perceived; the state of samādhi, or deep meditation.

UPANISHADS [*upaniṣad*]
(*lit.*, sitting close to; secret teachings) The inspired teachings, visions, and mystical experiences of the ancient sages of India. With immense variety of form and style, all of these scriptures (exceeding one hundred texts) give the same essential teaching: that the individual soul and God are one. *See also* VEDANTA.

VASISHTHA
The legendary sage and Guru of Lord Rama, who, in the *Yoga Vāsishtha,* answers Lord Rama's questions on the nature of life, death, and human suffering by teaching that the world is as you see it and that illusion ceases when the mind is stilled.

VEDANTA [*vedānta*]
(*lit.*, end of the Vedas) One of the six orthodox schools of Indian philosophy; usually identified as Advaita ("nondual") Vedanta, meaning that there is one supreme Principle that is the foundation of the universe. *See also* UPANISHADS.

VIJNANA BHAIRAVA
[*vijñānabhairava*]
An exposition of the path of yoga based on the principles of Kashmir Shaivism. Originally revealed in Sanskrit, probably in the seventh century, it is a compilation of 112 *dhāranās*, centering techniques, any of which can give the immediate experience of union with God. *See also* DHARANA.

YOGA [*yoga*]
(*lit.*, union) The spiritual practices and disciplines that lead a seeker to evenness of mind, to the severing of the union with pain, and through detachment, to skill in action. Ultimately, the path of yoga leads to the constant experience of the Self.

YOGA SUTRAS [*yogasūtra*]
A collection of aphorisms, written by the sage Patanjali in the fourth century, that expound different methods for the attainment of the state of yoga, or union, in which the movement of the mind ceases and the Witness of the mind rests in its own bliss.

YOGI [*yogi*]
1) One who practices yoga. 2) One who has attained perfection through yogic practices. *See also* YOGA.

Index

Absolute, 4
Aham brahmāsmi ("I am the Absolute"), 4
Anger, 17, 19
Apāna (exhalation), 11
Arjuna, 3, 17
Āsana (posture), 25-26, 27
Attainment, spiritual, 13, 15, 31, 37
Attention, turned within, 5, 24
Awakening, spiritual, 10-12, 27, 31
  See also Shaktipat
Awareness
  inner, 6-7
  mantra and, 24
  meditation and, 32, 34, 36, 37
  of Self, 3-4, 18, 21-22, 34
  of Shiva, 31-32

Bhagavadgītā, 3, 17, 24
Bistami, Hazrit Bayazid, 7-10
Bliss
  absolute, 14
  Consciousness and, 4
  meditation and, 10, 28, 31, 37
  shakti and, 27
  sleep and, 2
  See also Happiness
Blue Pearl, 29-30
Bodies, four, 28-29
Body, 3, 6, 10-11, 26, 28-30, 35
Books, 4
Breath, 11, 26, 30, 35
Brihajjābāla Upanishad, 10

Chakras, 11, 16
Chanting, 35
Chiti (Consciousness), 10, 20, 34
Clothing, for meditation, 35
Concentration, 5, 16
Consciousness, 10, 13-14
  all-pervasiveness of, 31-32
  contraction of, 20-21
  creation and, 11
  experience of, 8
  limitation of, 34
  meditation and, 35
  mind and, 20-21
  Self and, 4
Contentment, 2

Death, 10, 30
Delusion, 6
Dhāranā (concentration), 16
Disease, 5-6
Divinity, 2-3, 7-10, 32, 37
Dreams, 3, 6-7, 29
Duality, 30-31, 34

Ego, 17
Elements, 5
Enthusiasm, 27
Equality consciousness, 21-22
Experience
  of happiness, 1-2
  in meditation, 6, 28
  of Self, 4, 11-13, 15, 16-17

Faith, 27, 29, 32
Fantasies, 17
Fear, 36
Field, knower of, 3
Focus, 5, 16, 19, 24, 35

God
  all-pervasiveness of, 14, 31-32
  Blue Pearl and, 30
  experience of, 7-10, 12-13, 15
  longing for, 27
  mantra and, 23-24

To Deepen Your Meditation

by
Gurumayi Chidvilasananda

MEDITATION INSTRUCTIONS, VOLUME ONE

Gurumayi Chidvilasananda offers meditation instructions on this audio recording, which carries the listener gently and naturally into meditation. Her directions provide guidance in posture, breathing, and mantra repetition. "Begin your meditation with absolute conviction," Gurumayi tells us. "It is your right to perceive your own divine light within. It is completely possible for you to enter the cave of the heart. It is natural. It is inevitable. It will happen."

THE YOGA OF DISCIPLINE

"From the standpoint of the spiritual path," Gurumayi says, "the term *discipline* is alive with the joyful expectancy of divine fulfillment." In this book on practicing and cultivating discipline of the senses, Gurumayi shows us how this practice brings great joy.

SMILE, SMILE, SMILE!

Over the ages, many great saints and spiritual masters have offered their teachings in spontaneous poetry for the delight of their students. The verses in *Smile, Smile, Smile!* reflect this joyful tradition. Embroidering on the ideas and phrases of one of her talks, "Refresh your resolution. Smile at your destiny," Gurumayi illuminates the challenges and glories of spiritual life.

KINDLE MY HEART

The first of Gurumayi's books, this is an introduction to the classic themes of the spiritual journey, arranged thematically. There are chapters on such subjects as meditation, mantra, control of the senses, the Guru, the disciple, and the state of a great being.

MY LORD LOVES A PURE HEART

Fearlessness, reverence, compassion, freedom from anger — Gurumayi describes how these magnificent virtues are an integral part of our true nature. The list of virtues introduced is based on chapter 16 of the *Bhagavad Gītā.*

by
Swami Muktananda

WHERE ARE YOU GOING?

A comprehensive introduction to the teachings of Siddha Yoga meditation, this lively and anecdotal book explores the nature of the mind, the Self, and the inner power, as well as mantra, meditation, and the Guru.

PLAY OF CONSCIOUSNESS

In this intimate and powerful self-portrait, Baba describes his own journey to Self-realization, revealing the process of transformation he experienced under the guidance of his Guru, Bhagawan Nityananda.

MYSTERY OF THE MIND

"Thoughts control our experience," Baba tells us, "and if we can control the mind and the thought-waves it creates, we can make our world a paradise." In this fascinating discussion of the nature of the mind, Baba clearly reveals the yogic understanding of the power of letters, words, and images, and explains how this knowledge can help us make the mind our greatest friend.

I HAVE BECOME ALIVE

In this book, Baba shows us how to integrate the inner quest with the demands of contemporary life. He illumines such topics as spiritual discipline, the ego, marriage, parenting, experiencing love, and attaining God while embracing the world.

I AM THAT:
THE SCIENCE OF *HAMSA* FROM THE *VIJNANA-BHAIRAVA*

The secret of *Hamsa,* the awareness of the natural mantra of the breath, is revealed most clearly in verse 24 of the great Shaivite text *Vijñānabhairava.* In his commentary on this verse, Baba leads us step-by-step into the mysteries of this potent form of mantra repetition.

FOR FURTHER INFORMATION

Please write for the current list of publications in English, Hindi, Gujarati and Marathi to:

CHITSHAKTI BOOKSTORE,
GURUDEV SIDDHA PEETH,
P.O. GANESHPURI,
DIST THANE
MS 401 206